WORKBOOK FOR

I WILL TEACH YOU TO BE RICH

(A Guide to Ramit Sethi's Book)

Your Powerful Guide to Becoming Rich and Preserving It

THIS ONE WEEK OUTLINE WAS DEVELOPED TO HELP YOU.

➢ **The foremost thing is to find a person you can rely on to help you achieve your goals if you want to be successful.**

➢ **Be careful not to make any mistakes when filling out the vital forms displayed below.**

➢ **Consider each day's tip, task and prescription carefully.**

THINK ABOUT THEM MEDITATIVELY.

➢ **Everything you learned in the note should be written and meditated upon.**

Also, jot down your thoughts and feelings, as well as the obstacles you've come to terms with.

READ AND LISTEN TO
EVERYTHING
THAT IS BEING SAID
AND RECOMMENDED.

Without a doubt, adhere to
them.

IT WAS MADE TO BE
POSSIBLE.

Never doubt the fact that
you
can do it, and never give up
hope.

YOU'RE ALL SET TO STEP ON TO THE NEXT LEVEL!

Ensure that you fill out the Form below in its entirety.

DATE IT ALL BEGINS

DATE OF FINAL CONCLUSION (Usually 7 D ays from the starting Date)

Fill in the blanks with your name and email address:

FILL OUT YOUR AGE

———————————————————

———————————————————

It's not as difficult as you might
think, but don't take it for
granted and keep going.

Recommendations and
Tasks for the Day Don't End
That Day; Carry On and
Make Habits of Them.

DAY 1

INSIGHT

The first step to becoming rich remains your ability to set financial goals. Make a step by step plan and be willing to follow it up to the core.

WHAT YOU SHOULD IMBIBE TODAY

Make a plan to get rich. Outline the steps, businesses, actions to take and more. Make it realistic both in time and action.

DON'T FORGET...

He who fails to plan automatically
plans to fail.

MEDITATE

_____

_____

_____

_____

_____

_____

_____

_____

_____

_____

_____

_____

_____

_____

_____

_____

_____

_____

_____

_____

_____

_____

_____

_____

_____

_____

_____

_____

Your laid out goals are step by step ladders to success.

DAY 2

INSIGHT

Borrowed money can never automatically make you a rich man. Clearing off your debts is very important when it comes to the journey towards becoming successful.

WHAT YOU SHOULD IMBIBE TODAY...

Start making strong and sincere efforts to pay off all those you're owing. Ending the habit of borrowing money, always work with what you have.

<u>DON'T FORGET…</u>

Borrowed money is never your net
worth. Pay up your debts.

MEDITATE

_____

_____

_____

_____

_____

_____

_____

_____

_____

_____

_____

_____

_____

_____

_____

_____

_____

_____

_____

_____

_____

_____

_____

_____

_____

_____

Cultivate the habit of using what you have effectively without borrowing.

DAY 3

INSIGHT

Having a cushion (emergency fund storage) to cover up escalated expenses is indeed a good practice for this mission.

WHAT YOU SHOULD IMBIBE TODAY

Create an emergency fund account to save money for unforeseen but serious and unbudgeted expenses. This will save you from spending business money.

<u>DON'T FORGET...</u>

Business money should be treated as sacred; it should not be spent on other things.

MEDITATE…

_____

_____

_____

_____

_____

_____

_____

_____

_____

_____

_____

_____

_____

_____

_____

Spend only your profits in business.

DAY 4

INSIGHT

It's not all about making the money. Another very important hurdle remains your ability to keep it. This can only be solved by proper investment.

WHAT YOU SHOULD IMBIBE TODAY

Learn about how to make proper investments, find out the one that is best for you and do it. Make your money capable of working for you while you sleep.

<u>DON'T FORGET...</u>

No matter how big you think your money is, if you don't invest it'd finish sooner than you expect.

MEDITATE

_____
_____
_____
_____
_____
_____
_____
_____
_____
_____
_____
_____
_____
_____

_____

_____

_____

_____

_____

_____

_____

_____

_____

_____

_____

_____

_____

Investments remain the prime way to keep being rich.

DAY 5

INSIGHT

You need to be able to guard yourself against sudden but massive crash of business to be able to stay rich. This can only happen by diversifying your portfolio.

WHAT YOU SHOULD IMBIBE TODAY...

Make different investments across various fields, don't put all your eggs in one basket.

<u>DON'T FORGET</u>

Spread your wealth across different fields because anything can happen at any time.

MEDITATE

_____

_____

_____

_____

_____

_____

_____

_____

_____

_____

_____

_____

_____

_____

_____

_____

_____

_____

_____

_____

_____

_____

_____

_____

Don't ever presume!

<u>DAY 6</u>

<u>INSIGHT</u>

Reckless spending remains a very sure route to poverty. Learn to always spend your money intentionally and minimize costs.

<u>WHAT YOU SHOULD IMBIBE TODAY</u>

Spend only when necessary, stop extravagant lifestyle, save more and live below your means.

DON'T FORGET

The people that prompt you to spend
so much in order to impress them
don't really care about you.

MEDITATE

_____

_____

_____

_____

_____

_____

_____

_____

_____

_____

_____

_____

_____

_____

Don't destroy your life just
so that they'd feel you.

DAY 7

INSIGHT

Having a side hustle is a behavior adopted by most people who build money and maintain it. This is different from investment. Have a second sure job that'd help you fund your business, savings and lifestyle.

WHAT YOU SHOULD IMBIBE TODAY

Move out and find a profitable side hustle to add to your job.

<u>DON'T FORGET</u>

Side hustles save you from more things than you can imagine.

MEDITATE

_____

_____

_____

_____

_____

_____

_____

_____

_____

_____

_____

_____

_____

_____

_____

_____

_____

_____

_____

_____

_____

_____

_____

_____

_____

_____

_____

Find a side hustle today.

YOU'VE FINISHED WITHTHIS ONE WEEK GUIDE. KEEP UP WITH IT.

POSITIVE RESULT COMES WITH IT.

Show Love to people by giving them copies of this.

_____

_____

_____

_____

_____

_____

_____

_____

_____

_____

_____

_____

_____

_____

_____

_____

BYE!

Each time you're deviating, return to this!

Made in United States
Troutdale, OR
01/01/2024

16597308R00022